MW00873855

Edited by: Susan Frohnsdorff, Charleston, SC

Marketing Consultant: Shelia Murph, Somerset, NJ

ebsite and Graphic design by: Fa'lon Thomas, Raleigh, NC

Cover Photo: The Battery, Charleston, SC

Back Cover Photo: Kiawah Beach, Kiawah Island, SC

DEDICATED TO

MY CHILDREN,

CHARLES, FA'LON AND RICARDO;

TO MY FIVE SIBLINGS;

AND TO MY DEAR FRIENDS,

WHO LOVED ME BEFORE,

DURING, AND BEYOND THE TEARS

Contents

Introduction

It is written, "Weeping may endure for the night, but joy cometh in the morning." (Psalms 30:5 KJV)

In the aforementioned scripture, David praises God for His deliverance. The entire fifth verse reads, "For His anger endures but a moment; in His favor is life: weeping may endure for a night, but joy cometh in the morning."

On this journey called life, I have wept many nights. I have sought joy and peace like a nomad lost in the desert digging with his bare hands in the sand underneath a hot sun for water that did not exist.

And then, it was a day like none other. I cried out to my God who sits high and looks low, "Please,

Father, restore to me a place of peace where joy abides." Somewhere between my emptiness and my broken heart, I heard these words, "You are Joy."

From that moment forth, when someone asked my name, I said, "My name is Joy." The transition was seamless, uplifting and, more often than not, healing. To be clear, my mother gave me the birth name Joyce, which has served me well; however, when life drained my soul and wounded my spirit, my Heavenly Father reminded me that I am Joy. The word alone seems to bring a smile all dressed up in some form of healing. How could it be, that something so simplistic can be more precious than gold?

As you read my collection of short stories and poems laced with hills and valleys, pain and gratefulness, I pray above all that you know there is a place Beyond the Tears, and finally there is JOY.

Beyond the Tears

Often, I dance with inner fear or the concept that
being trapped supersedes a

mental and emotional state.

The reality is, trapped does not necessarily
constitute no or slow movement.

I have found that I move a great deal while being
trapped.

I move towards a place, and space that has no
name.

Could it be my destiny coming in the distance to
meet, and greet me?

Could it be an endless pursuit of an illusion that
I dressed up with fine linens, silk

and pearls, draped in a tiara that reads
happiness?

Indeed, I hear the sounds of the water fall
through the cries of my loneness.

I see the white cumulus clouds that play catch,
hide-go-seek and blind man's bluff

with the sun.

I glanced and saw the beautiful roses that grew
in spite of my arrogance, and total

neglect.

I look in my mirror, and clearly see signs of age,
traces of beauty and burdens of

duty.

Suddenly, the sun begins to shine ever so
brightly, as if it were laughing at me all

the while.

Silly me, there is an exit, there is a tomorrow,
there is an eternity; of this I am certain as I move

Beyond the Tears.

The River too Wide to Cross

There is a river far too wide to cross.

It is never wet, except for random tears,

It is never ever aqua or blue.

Turbulence is at home there, where no peaceful ships dare to roam,

The River too Wide to Cross is the place I often call home…..

Old Men on Benches

Old men on benches,

What a plenty they often have to say,

Swapping lies over checkers, cheating on chess.

Did they stop to smell a summer breeze

or hear the sparrow sing?

Chuck rocks across the creek, or hear the church bells ring?

A few dollars in the bank, not much else to show;

Moth-eaten pinstriped suits,

With not a single place to go,

Old men on benches, will I someday be like you,

Whittling away the hours, claiming there's nothing else to do?

Arm in the Air

Little more than a silhouette in the distance, brown shirt,
black pants, hair pulled back in a bushy

Brussels sprout poof that had to be contained by something
or another.

The distance prevented me from knowing her age, twenties
perhaps, with slim figure, upright breast,

and brown skin, one slow dance darker than her shirt,

squeaky, semi-rusted railroad tracks, rotted cross ties to my
right and in front of her.

She held that arm up in the air such a long, long time, it
seemed.

Didn't occur to me she was greeting all the passengers on the
fast-moving train, not just me.

I hope she knew I would have waved back –

were it not for the swift pace #73 from Charlotte headed East
was moving ...

judging from the constant bellowing of that train whistle
blowing, disrupting an anxious

passenger's silence, we might have been just a bit behind
schedule.......

How grand it would be if the lady with the arm far too long in the air knew just how

grateful I was for her much needed unconditional wave.

Silent Winds Emerge

There is a Wind that has been raging

Deep, so very deep in my unsettled soul.

How long, you ask, have I endured such turbulence?

For so long a time, I don't really know.

What I know for sure is,

Today is my day of bliss, because a Silent Wind shall Emerge,

Propelling me to heights of rest.

Just as Soon As

Just as soon as I decide that the cares of life are far too heavy for me to bear,

A butterfly frolics before me,

Displaying her beauty and majesty in that multicolored overcoat.

Just as soon as my pillow is soaked with tears of heartache, disappointment and pain,

The sun glistens and beckons my soul to try just another day.

Just as soon as failed dreams and trouble on every side overtake me,

And smother every hope for tomorrow,

I catch a glimpse of a child's smile and hear the Melody of the bluebird in flight.

Just as soon as darkness overtakes me,

Daylight embraces me and I know in the silence of my soul that everything will be alright.

Ripples Across the Pond

The journey has been long, grueling, life-
threatening and hopelessly unkind,

Salt-baked tears were often my portion,
while I nodded with a faux smile at the
perpetrators,

forever fighting that which is right and
just.

I questioned the motives of my aching
heart beating un-rhythmically, while
shouting threats that it

would quit, I talk back to my suspicious
eyes that lied to me far more than once.

It makes no sense, my inability to feel the
rain,

Some from afar off, postulating with a
bird's-eye view, say the heat of the sun

was beating down on me for so long it undoubtedly baked my brain.

They haven't a clue, wading in their own knee deep pit, that I made a pact with the wind today.

The deal is, I would strip myself from all unwanted residue and then ride the back of the East

Wind to a

place called forgiveness, making room for peace showering me from head to toe.

Any uncircumscribed noise that

Scurries to remind me would forever remain behind me with an engraved headstone that reads, Ripples Across the Pond.

Selected Memory

You remember that red negligee with smooth silk ribbon,
pretending to be a tie,

I remember thick silence, far too deep to cut through,
forgetting to ask why.

You remember uncooked dinners, I remember saying, "So,
what the heck,"

You remember giving me furs, diamonds, tangible earthly
treasures untold.

I remember longing for you to touch me in a place and space
beyond your ability to know.

I remember crying into my pillow, trusting it not to tell a soul.

You remember embracing a new love, not even concerned
with the old.

I remember robbing my tomorrow with empty thoughts and
weighted sorrow.

Finally, I remember

Somethings we just need to forget!

My Heart Aches

My heart is sorely heavy, it aches for the child

It screams for the injustice done that has marred their smile

My dry tears are wet rivers that seem to have no end

My unanswered questions lead me back to places that I've been

The beautiful yellow and black butterfly that frolics about

Renders only momentary pleasure, all the while I want to shout

My heart is sorely heavy it aches for the child

Whose innocence was robbed, stripped, stolen and thrust

Just to satisfy the sick minded adult with untamed lust

Their faces are far too many, their pain far too wide

We told them they could always trust us, when all we did was lied

My heart is sorely heavy; it aches for the child.......

Some Days

Some days I spend far too much time in
yesterday

Stretching, reaching, yearning for her delight

Continuously by passing, omitting, deleting
and hiding

from the thorns of yesterday's roses....

Day Break

Day break arrived in spite of the rubble of my shame,

Despite bloodshed, laughter and ongoing pain,

Day break arrived on a chariot, escorted by a cloud,

A few confused eagles, a giant snake and a tiny sparrow,

The good news is, day break arrived!

The Babysitter

Babysitting his bout with sheer insanity, I found myself whittling away my hours in the strangest of places. This time, its downtown Raleigh on a Saturday night, parked at the corner of Fayetteville and East Hargett.

The friendly mid-May breeze had that flag blowing on the Capitol Building at a steady, rhythmic pace.

The man across the street in front of the CVS Pharmacy breathed into his saxophone, resulting in a smooth jazz that hugged the air like a sweet-smelling fragrance after a heavy rain. For some odd reason, mostly women stopped and dropped a little something into his saxophone case that lay spread-eagled on the ground.

The abundance of taxi cabs whipping to and fro, drivers must have been thinking this was New York City instead of Raleigh, North Carolina.

Somehow, I just knew this was the perfect place to park while he went into what he called a Venue, chasing the latest frequent dream of being a Dee Jay. He said it only cost two dollars for him to get in. It was priceless for me to believe he would find peace from those

noisy voices rolling around inside his head.

Those voices were hell-bent on trying to destroy

his life, and there I sat in his car waiting

patiently for him to go and dance with the

possibility that peace of mind would find him.

     Numbly I sat, watching all those young

folks, most of whom looked well under half my

age. What more could a mother do to save her

son from self-destruction, and all that noise

rolling around inside his head? Clearly, they

have him levitating way above basic common

sense.

Not sure how long I marinated in my own reverie when a clumsy thought intruded, and I wondered just how much that man on the corner, breathing such glorious melody into that saxophone makes on a Saturday night such as this?

It used to be 10:00 p.m., now its 1:15 a.m., and I am still sitting. Horns still blowing, no longer a nuisance to my ears like before, young folks now ambling with a swagger or stagger that appeared to be first cousin to inebriation, perhaps too much of first one thing and then another.

Downtown Raleigh was soon to shut down, only so long it could pretend to be New York City.

I asked him to be back by 1:30, he'll be pretty close to that time, I know 'cause he doesn't want to ruffle my feathers, knowing I'm too darn close to the edge myself.

Indeed

Looking back over her shoulder with a glance that had long since removed

The pain of looking back,

I could tell in the quick simple gesture that she had

Made peace with yesterday,

Sort of put it in its place, stripping it of all that bully power it

Used to have, all the while robbing her of sunsets and blue skies,

I saw an as-a-matter-of-fact look in her face, which was the

Color of honey or charcoal, or Karo syrup, nutmeg, caramel, or peaches and cream,

Her hue mattered not, what mattered was the notion that she had given her

Wings permission to fly,

Suddenly, she glances in my direction, proudly focused on sharing

Her many years of truth,

I look deep into her eyes, full of wisdom and seeing many lies afar

Off, yet up close,

For a brief moment I thought I saw a bruise from a black eye,

I urgently dismissed that thought, no, it could not be; if her journey

Included residuals from countless battles she hid them in her pocket

Or some other inconspicuous place,

Her lips were thick or thin or thick and thin,

Coveting years, miles and journeys, she muttered nor uttered not a word,

Time had anointed her far too wise to speak,

I saw her more now, or perhaps now is when I begin to see,

Indeed!

The Yard Boy

I watched as he manicured the lawn, pruned the trees and dug the weeds, sweat never crossing his brow.

"Yard boy," I cried from my cushioned seat, blowing the final puff of smoke from my elongated cigarette, smelling the fragrance of the rose he had just cut for me. "Have you any dreams, Yard Boy"?

He glanced up, never disrupting the rhythm of the lawn trimmers. "Dreams, Madam? I have dreams aplenty."

Placing my iced tea on the table, positioning myself from the rays of the hot afternoon sun, I retorted, "Yard Boy, what dreams have you?"

"Does Madam wish to know my dreams"?

Feeling myself becoming vexed, trying desperately to avoid intimidation, "Yard Boy," I vociferated, "stop what you're doing and stand before me."

Laying the trimmers on the grass delicately, he walked the short distance to my veranda. His coal black eyes reflected wisdom as his stride adorned self-worth. "Indeed, Yard Boy will tell Madam of his dreams, only if Madam can bear to hear."

I could no longer control my emotions as my voice betrayed my plot. "I want your dreams and I want them now."

With the grace of a baron he began to speak.

"Do forgive me Madam, I will tell you of my dreams. I dream of Madam and then I weep."

"Why, Yard Boy, do you dream of me and weep? I have reaped the fruits of my father's toil, I eat the best of the cow's beef, I drink the finest wine from the German harvest, and my bath is filled with oil. You, Yard Boy, turn ash in the sun, all the while beautifying my existence for a fee that

26

affords you only day-old bread, and you weep for me? Weep no longer you foolish boy."

As he humbly began to speak, I noticed for the first time the life that existed beyond those coal black eyes, kinky hair, and dried-out skin. It was as if he had waited a lifetime for this very moment.

"Madam, if in all your glory you can answer Yard Boy one single riddle, I will weep for you no more."

"Yard Boy, first you test my patience and now you dare test my wit. Surely, your intellect is inferior to mine. However, if I can answer your riddle you must surrender your earnings for the entire day."

Displaying a victorious smile he spoke. "Madam, I will relinquish my earnings but ... if you cannot answer, may I sit with you in your splendor and bake my brain in the hot sun no more?"

I glared at his dirty, torn overalls and laughed at the blackness of his skin. What a proud boy, I thought. Compared to my nobility this peasant has not a chance. I kindly nodded my head in agreement and sat back in my chair. "Yard Boy, if I cannot answer your riddle, you shall share my splendor forevermore."

He flashed the largest smile with teeth as bright as the midday sun, and then he took a deep breath and kind of shook his head in a condescending way.

"Madam, can you tell Yard Boy the meaning of a blade of grass?"

Stunned, I sat upright, managing to capture a quick view of the mountains in the distance. I reached for a cigarette and accepted his offer to give me a light.

"Yard Boy," I said with a defeated smile, "tomorrow I will not sit alone."

Yesterday

Yesterday often weighs me down,

Like high heels on swollen feet,

Like thoughts from unpleasant dreams,

And dreams that shall never come to pass.

Yesterday tells lies, she robs you of today, and shields tomorrow's sun.

I often dance with her for countless hours and hum to that pathetic,

Yet familiar tune.

The Ocean Calls

Some days the Ocean beckons me and calls me by name,

He often has secrets to tell or a message from above,

I respect each thunderous wave or turbulent sun-kissed ray,

His smell is fresh like lavender, it tickles me into an anxious oblivion,

Where I am at home with constant laughter, ignoring drops of earthly pretense.

When the Ocean Calls, I find peace as far as my courageous heart can see,

He fuses all lifelong fragmentations,

Cements them with the gentle touch of hope, promise and possibility,

Some days the Ocean beckons me,

and calls me by name.

The Other Black Man

In the center of his weakness

He gives birth to strength

In the shadow of his emptiness stands

Hope for a better way

In the unspoken screams

Gentle rivers flow

In the pain and disappointment

Generations emerge from the dust

He knows no river he cannot cross

He knows no tears that the sunlight dare not dry

When hell was all around

He knew heaven was his home...........

The Wrapping

She wrapped herself between so much hate until it stuck like peanut butter on light bread.

From afar off I would say, she picked up a little here and a little there until she was totally consumed with that nasty thing.

I'm sure she never saw her world unraveling like a wad of yarn caught in a cat's mouth, racing a million miles per minute, going nowhere in particular.

Up close she wore a smile, most days, shrouded in colors of purple, blue and gray, bleeding profusely from her wounded soul.

I tried so many times to reach her or perhaps save her from some of that ungodly pain.

The trouble is or was, words never came my way.

I often wanted to touch her with just a hug or a gentle pat, but all that wrapped-up hate seemed to leave freezer burns in the very thought.

She would look at me with that empty look seeking for someone to blame; here's the thing, I was not about to wear that garment for nobody, not for love nor money, far too heavy a load.

I did manage to do something though; one day when the sun was bright and the timing seemed right I said out loud, like I was talking to myself, "You know healing is a quiet thing, never really know the moment it occurs, just have to shed that junk one step at a time until freedom is your home."

With a timorous glance she looked my way, kind of gave me a grin, as if she were hoping

What I spoke was true.

Roar of the Gods

Suddenly, the clouds assumed a foreign artistry;

Their new formation puzzled even the wisest of men.

And then, the Yellow man, Red man, Jew, Gentile, Muslim,

And Hindu dropped to their knees upon this wicked earth.

Their cries could be heard from the mountain tops;

Mercy, Mercy was their plea.

The rich man disembarking from his yacht, fearing the turbulence of the

Rebelling sea, vociferating for his chauffeur, whose loyalties were only to himself.

The rose on the vine began to wither; there was no one to relish her beauty

Nor appreciate the sweetness of her smell.

Fear, Decadence and Repentance permeated the air, Death perfumed the Universe.

In the distance, far more audible than the pain, I heard a child's voice echoing ferociously

Through the confused and bewildered trees,

"Mommy, is this the end?"

She Cries from the Ashes

I let it die soon after I discovered the painstaking effort it would take to nurture it.

At that very moment the journey would be a lonely one,

Many years of false hopes and public deceptions.

I often wonder if it were a slow, debilitating death or stabbing in the dark,

Listening for the sound of profuse bleeding.

My wondering took me even further; it took me to a place so foreign

And far beyond rhyme or reason.

It took me to his world, where deception seemed to be the norm and deceit status quo.

A world where the King aligned himself with the enemy to dethrone the queen.

How could he not see? How could he not have known?

How he leaves blood on the floor every place he has gone?

Lord knows, it shall never make sense to

Me, I'll never comprehend the game.

What I will do is rise above the ashes, I'll shake the dust
from many years of unwanted residue,

And glide on any of the joy from years gone by.

Alas, from the depths of my spirit and the core of my
soul I'll proclaim to the heavens, "I shall

Leave my bed of ashes, replace it with beauty

And cast my tears to the wind."

When Silence Speaks

I eagerly await your voice, yearning for a word,

Feeling like a child in a busy marketplace disconnected from my mother's gentle touch,

My world spinning a million miles per hour in slow motion,

Far too many false and empty smiles,

Lies, deceit and deception oozing from every pore,

Too many our reached hands too eager to drain the life from me, leaving my derailed dreams

Splattered like roadkill on life's highway,

Yet, Lord you are silent.

Silent like the long lonely night, void of lantern or moonlight,

Silent like yesterday's pain that left invisible bruises and altered recollections of truth,

Silent like my tear-drenched pillow, promising to never tell a soul,

Silent like the hunger pains waging war against my empty spirit, promising a slow death,

Silent like the gentle touch of a newborn baby, heart
beating, blood flowing,

Brain dead from the mother's womb, no real life there.

Somehow, sifting through the noisy fog, I manage to feel
your presence,

I see your invisible eye through my desperate and needy
heart.

Yes, oh yes, you are protecting me, guiding, carrying me,
just as you hold the moon in space,

Lace the sky with playful clouds that dance all the day
with the sun.

You are here, here you are, in the summer breeze and
whispering wind,

Amid wild horses feasting along the mountainside,
obeying rhythmic sounds, refusing to be

Tamed. Yet, you are silent.

There is an unexplainable calm that covers me like dew
embellishing the earth, announcing

Morning's approach.

I cautiously monitor my every move, making sure I am
not circling the block.

In the quiet of my dilemma, while wondering which way
to go, I am somehow able to rest in the

belly of the whale. Seems this is the most important time,
crucial in every way.

I rest upon the window seat, counting leaves from the old
oak tree.

Suddenly, the bluebird appears along the pristine ledge,
bodacious, yet deliberate in his arrival,

Briefly eyeballing me as he briskly turns to fly away.

"Trust Me," were the two words that he uttered.

Seems Trust Me is all your silence had to say.

After the Storm

Just as sure as the sun promised to rise

again, there is always an "after the storm."

Sometimes after the storm the leaves on the

old oak tree move so slowly from side to

side,

Holding on to each movement like two lovers

dancing the two-step with rhythmic beats

only they can hear.

Depending on the magnitude of the storm,

the after can bring forth a sense of relief or,

41

Worst case, an empty anticipation of another

storm waiting patiently beyond an aqua sky

and

Restrained clouds.

How marvelous it would be to retreat like the

jaybird to some unknown place at the first

inclination of

An impending storm, and come out singing

just as if nothing ever happened at all.

The quiet of the storm aftermath can be a tad

bit eerie, like tiptoeing through unfamiliar

pebbled places in shoes

That don't fit your feet.

42

I have noticed, though, the panic that

preceded the storm; no matter grand or

slight, it fades into a calm

That is third cousin to a respite or Sunday

morning, sipping sweet tea on a country

porch.

My pulse is now synchronized with the flow

of the heartbeat after the storm, someplace

in the

Neighborhood of normalcy, where it should

have taken abode in the first place.

In spite of all that I am for sure, wise as

Marylou's granny, that I learn over and over

again after each and

Every storm that I journeyed through

How to ride on the back of mighty strong

winds with ribbons of Hope holding down my

Hair.........

Was That Me

I saw her approaching, peddling her pink bike with white
straw basket,

In a steady rhythmic speed,

Not too fast, not too slow, just enough to keep it moving.

As she approached, within an arm's-length distance, I saw
her gray hair,

Her face painted with wrinkles, while her neck co-signed
every lived year.

Our eyes swiftly met, her look pensive; void of a smile or
friendly grin, I gave as much as

I got, as she peddled by. If I had to guess, it would be that she
was riding on this college campus

Wondering where the years went and how rapidly they had
done so. I was visiting my daughter on the

college campus, wondering where the years were going.

I suspect what we had in common, the stranger cycling and
me walking, was the fact that we both

Knew for sure that there were fewer years in front of us than
those already spent;

It appeared she had

at least a twenty-year head start on me.

I was suddenly oblivious to the speed in my pace,

probably to validate that energy and youthfulness were still my friend.

The wind whistled, as it passed gently through my hair.

My sassy step moved in the direction of a sprint.

I shut all that noise from those young folks rambling around this college campus,

that old cycling Stranger afar off in the distance now;

I smelled tomorrow thick in the air, accompanied with the

Weight of unanswered wonder,

Was That Me?

Gentle Brisk Fall Day

Walking in the woods, listening to the sound of seasons changing,

Leaves falling all over the place,

Blanketing my every step with vibrant colors, crimson, yellow, sage and two tones,

The crisp sound of crunch, crunch, crunch coming from leaves that must have been among

The first to fall.

Some random North Carolina bird chirping all loud in the tall tree,

Offering just a bit of consolation for my heavy heart, which was trying desperately

To lose weight.

This here wooden bench I rested upon, strangely placed amid nature's beauty and splendor,

Seems to be telling me something, as I can now feel the creases of wood against my sedentary

Mindset. Truth is, it wasn't until the acorn fell from the sneaky tree deeply planted behind me and

Landed upon my head that I embraced the notion,

It's time to move on!

Even the Oak Tree Knows

The stately oak tree, with all his strength and nobility, covets many secrets, wishes and dreams. Who else knew of the young woman, who wore her shame like a crocheted shawl draped around hunched shoulders, carrying a lad that was truly not her own? It was a time when the young ladies waited with baited breath for a man to take her hand in marriage. Heaven help her if she reached 25 without partaking in such an auspicious occasion. She would be deemed an old maid, a spinster, and cast down like the runt of the litter among purebreds.

The old oak tree saw her coming in the cool of the night, when crickets sang, and the possums, rabbits and raccoons thrust about. She quietly approached, using the full moon and a small lantern as her light. As she reached the old oak tree, she noticed a stump the hunters used to rest upon. The old oak tree watched suspiciously as she carefully placed her lantern on the ground and kneeled in front of the stump. She placed her hands together, facing the brightness of the full moon, and began to pray, "Lord, send me a man. Lord, send me a man." The old bug-eyed hooting owl, with his noisy self, began to hoot, "whooo, whooo, whooo, whooo." The young lady heard the sound, believing it to be a question directed to her and her alone and replied, "Anybody, Lord. I don't care who." The stately old oak chuckled within himself and never told a soul.

~~~~~~~~~~~~~~~~~~~~~~

It was a day like no other; the sun caressed the aqua blue sky like a mother viewing her newborn for the first time. The early birds sent messages filled with love, one to another. Most of the other trees had begun to shed their leaves, awaiting the arrival of a Michigan winter. The stately old oak tree gave no thought to such a natural phenomenon. He knew that time brings on a change, and with that change, there was truly nothing new under the sun.

~~~~~~~~~~~~~~~~~~~~~~

"Look. Look there," he whispered to the oak tree that stood ten feet beside him.

"What? What now?" responded the oak tree, who was not nearly as alert, although he was, at least, fifty years younger than the first.

"Never you mind," replied the stately oak tree, deciding, like the eagle, to soar alone.

The beat of their stride could be heard crunching against the many green, red and yellow leaves that blanketed the ground like dew in the morning on a lily pond. She stopped and rested her back upon the oak tree and took a deep breath as if this were a familiar place. She appeared young, yet not as young as it may have seemed. He touched her cheek gently with the tips of fingers from a laborer's hand. He spoke in an audible tone, since, clearly, there was no one around to hear.

"I promise we'll get married just as soon as I come back from the war."

Her single tear betrayed her silent thoughts, "This life within me will surely not wait." Walking away, hand in hand, the stately old oak tree heard her say, "My mother always told me that the devil trusted the turkey and he flew."

The man laughed, she sighed, and the stately old oak tree knew that for her, there would be many a dark lonely day.

~~~~~~~~~~~~~~~~~~~~~~~~~~~~~~~~~~~

The afternoon sun beat down with a vengeance, having no mercy on beast nor man. Late August in Michigan could be hotter than Ned's wife when she found out about Sadie. The stately old oak tree knew he would have guests today, if only to seek refuge from the angry sun. School returned early from summer vacation that year.

Alas, off in the distance he could hear them coming, running so very fast, close to the speed of light. "My lord," he said, speaking to no one in particular, since he and the oak tree ten feet beside him had not spoken in many years. "Why in the world aren't they in school on a day like today?" The two young boys stopped to rest, or perhaps just catch their breath for a while. One sat upon the old stump that many knew as a resting place. The other leaned against the old oak tree, digging a hole in the dirt with the toe of worn out sneakers. "Is this your first time?" the boy perched on the stump asked the other. "No," he replied, wiping the sweat from his brow and sounding somewhat sad. "Well?" came the second question.

"Well what?" was the reply, in a tone that reflected the beginning of annoyance. "Well, how often do you do it?"

This time he didn't wait for a reply but rattled on. "My dad would skin me alive if he ever found out," shaking his head as if he just realized the magnitude of his words. The labored silence of the moment gave way only to the birds' synchronized melody. "I never knew my dad; he was killed in the war. I've seen pictures though, and read letters he sent my mom."

They planned to get married just as soon as he returned from the war, just never made it back.

"Oh man, that must be rough."

"It's okay, 'cept mom works all the time. If she's not in church she's working or looking for more work. She said life's not fair, but God is good."

"Do you believe in God?"

"Yes, I know there is a God. I see him in the sunrise or the moon that lights the night. I feel him embrace me when I'm sad and all alone. I smell him in the flower garden or grapevine that grows so free. I taste him in the tears I shed for a father I never knew."

"Wow, man you're deep."

"Yeah, right. That's why we're out here skipping school and throwing away the only opportunity that we might have to rise above our pain." The two boys shared the silence, one waiting for the other to speak.

"I think I better get to school before my dad finds out."

"I'm with you."

The old oak tree was proud and swaying his many branches from side to side, rendering a cool breeze in the midst of the sun's relentless heat.

~~~~~~~~~~~~~~~~~~~~~~~~~~~~~~~~~~~~~

Many years had come and gone; so very much had changed. The area where the oak tree now stood was nothing but an urban lot where few trees remained. He was sure it was her approaching in the distance, though time had colored her hair and wrinkled her skin. The cane that supported her brittle bones separated her from the young boy she was with. "What are you looking for, Grandma?"

"Oh, son, I know this is the spot, although many things have changed." Looking around, she stopped at the old oak tree.

The oak tree could tell she was dancing with thoughts of years gone by.

The child's words abruptly brought her back. "Granny, my daddy said you're the strongest and most wonderful mother in the world."

The old lady smiled. "Is that a fact?"

"Yeah, and my daddy said he would not be a successful man today if it were not for you."

"You don't say."

"Yeah, and my daddy said you moved heaven and earth to feed, school and clothe him, and he said you did it all by yourself. Granny, will I grow up to be as wonderful as you and as great as my dad?"

The old lady bent down, hugged the boy, and smiled. "Well, son, there is no doubt about it.

"Everybody, who is anybody, can look at you and tell.

"In fact, my son,

"Even the oak tree knows."

The Young Saint

There was once a young lady whom the Lord saved from a life of sin. She became a beacon of light in the midst of a lost and dying world. Everyone who crossed her path, be he saved or unsaved, was embraced by the love of the Lord within this young lady.

There was also an old mother of the church who could be found sitting in the same church pew every service down through the years. When the preacher preached, it was her Amen and Praise Gods that could be heard above all others.

One day the old church mother sent a message to the young lady that she wanted to have a few words with her. So, after church the young lady went to the front of the church and there she found the old church mother sitting in the seat that she had occupied year after year, service after service.

The young lady looked down at the old mother, finding it difficult not to notice her crisp, pure white dress, her salt-and-pepper hair which was more salt than pepper, slicked back in a neat bun; she smelled as if she wore a perfume that was gently laced with lavender on a spring day.

After what seemed like a few days short of an eternity, the young lady began to speak. "Mother you have words for me?"

The old church mother looked up at the young lady, patting the empty seat next to her, indicating that she should have a seat. After clearing her throat the old church mother began to speak.

"Yes, baby," touching the young lady's hand with kind strokes of wisdom. She seemed to look off into the distance searching for just the right thing to say.

"Baby, you know I've been in the way a long, long time. In fact, the Lord saved me back in 1949, filled me with His Spirit and that with a burning fire.

"And baby, I walk and talk with the Lord from sun up to sun down.

"Yes, baby, I've been in the way a many years now.

"Baby, listen to this. I believe the Lord could use you if you just take off some of that lipstick, loose the hem from that dress a few inches, and when you cut those fingernails try to use clear finger nail polish.

"Yes, I believe the Lord could use you."

The young lady, who had been listening so attentively, reverently embracing every word, turned to the old mother with love and humility in her eyes, and began to speak.

"Mother, I've asked the Lord to come into my life and forgive me of my sins and save my soul and that he did.

I asked the Lord to fix me up and he did. I asked the Lord to clean me up and he took out my stony heart and gave me a heart of flesh.

"I asked the Lord to make me just like Him and he gave me the fruits of the spirit.

"So now, Mother, you know I do indeed share the love of the Lord throughout the highways and hedges. I feed the hungry, I clothe the naked, I pray for the bound, bless God; I've even been known to lay hands on the sick and through God they have recovered.

"Mother I realize that you have been in "the way" a many years and if you think the Lord forgot to do something in me I'll go right now back to the altar and fall on my knees."

The old mother said nothing as she watched the young lady kneel at the altar and audibly begin to pray.

"Lord, when I was drowning in a sea of sin you came along just in time and taught me how to swim.

"Lord when I was hungry your word became the food that sustained me.

"Lord, when I was thirsty it was you who was the living water.

"Lord, when my father and mother forsook me it was you who took me in.

"Lord, when I was friendless it was you who became my friend who was closer than a brother.

"Now, Lord Jesus, I know that I will walk with you until I die or until you come again. I am reminded of your word which clearly states, 'Now unto Him who is able to keep me from falling' …

"So, with you I have no reason to fall.

"But Lord, dear Lord, whatever you do, please don't ever let me be "IN THE WAY."

The Saga of Kobe Cat

Kobe Cat, with his smooth black slick coat, underbelly white stripe, and large deep set almond-shaped eyes, was literally born on the Wrong Side of the Track. Which really made no sense to him; after all it was the same distance to get from this side or that. Oh sure, the cats on the other side lived in big Victorian-styled homes and their parents drove big rides, with names like Cadillac, Mercedes and Beamer. But Kobe always felt the love of his mother and brother; after all, a home is where love abides. For sure no house made of wood, brick, or mortar or a ride with funny names and fancy emblems could compare with that.

Every day he would leave for school about the same time his mother left to go to work at the hot, steamy laundry, where she stood on all fours, eight, nine, often even ten hours a day, folding and pressing sheets for the Cat Town Hospital. She would always give him a hug, remind him to hold his head high, never slump his back and always look the other cats straight in the eye.

His brother Souly, on the other hand was a good big brother, as good as he was able to be. Cause you see, instead of going straight to school, Souly would step boldly out the back and head straight to the old abandoned shack at the end of the track.

Souly cat had a strong rugged gray coat, intertwined with sprinkles of black that appeared to be an afterthought. Oh man, he had a walk, a rhythm, a stride like none other. Man old man Souly, would take a step leading off with the front left paw, dip a bit and thrust with the right shoulder, head held high, cool and noble, some of the cats called him, " cool breeze," it fit him ever so well.

Kobe loved his big brother with an unconditional love. His deep set almond eyes saw and embraced only the goodness in his big brother cat. That said, Kobe knew that Souly would show up at school after going to that abandoned shack at the end of the track with a different step, eyes squinting, red and glazed, a silly smile, cap turned inside out, unable to focus; kinda like being in a daze is how Kobe would describe it in his mind.

Just the thought … if Mama ever saw him in such a state she would choke him so hard everyone would hear his meows on both sides of the track. Nevertheless, Souly had a big heart and Kobe knew the love between them was sacred, far beyond special, and unspeakably deep.

Here's the thing: Souly was only a year and a half older than Kobe, but he had wisdom far beyond his years, in a strange kinda way.

He would say to Kobe, "I have three lessons for you to learn, but those lessons will be more costly than diamonds, more brilliant than rubies, and more precious than gold."

Day in and day out Souly would say to Kobe,

Lesson number 1 – "Watch what cats do, not what cats say."

"Yeah, yeah," Kobe would reply. Truth is, Kobe figured Souly was just meowing gibberish, the result of far too many visits behind the abandoned shack at the very end of the track.

Day after day Souly would bellow, bordering on crazy, "Hey Bro cat, lesson number 2 – "The devil trust the turkey and he flew." Then he would chuckle, in a way that only Souly could chuckle.

Kobe would reply his same reply. "Souly, you are forever meowing loud and saying nothing."

But deep, way deep down in his soul he knew the lessons of life that Souly shared with only him meant something, something very special, something very important, perhaps even life-altering.

Truth is, he just couldn't put his paw on what exactly it was they meant.

~~~~~~~~~~~~~~~~~~~

Days and seasons came and went, spring turned to summer, summer turned to fall, fall turned to winter. Mama's hair turned white mixed with black. Kobe thought he heard tell that it was called "salt and pepper."

Her tail began to sag a bit as well, but she was still the most beautiful mother cat in the land. Heck, and that included all the mother cats from the Right or Wrong Side of the Track.

Kobe used to hear the other mother cats in the row houses whisper, "Oh poor Lottie Cat, she says her husband died, but he just left and never came back."

Mama knew what the whispers were; she never bothered to set them straight. She would just continue to smile day after day.

Kobe, on the other hand, heavily adorned with righteous indignation, was eager to set them straight, but Mama Cat would say, "Kobe, never chase behind a lie, it's a long and winding road leading to another lie. But, on the other paw, truth can stand any storm. In fact, when the storm is over, truth will still be standing."

Kobe would scratch his head and under his breath say, "I guess Souly got his innate wisdom from Mama." The truth remained, neither of them made much sense to him sometimes.

~~~~~~~~~~

Life went on, like life seems to do. Nothing much changed in the row houses on the Wrong Side of the Track.

Souly managed to graduate high school, albeit only barely.

It always seemed Souly was headed nowhere in particular, but someplace, just in case. He decided to join the Cat Army; only thing that troubled Mama was, our country was fighting a war in a strange land. It made Mama Cat seem a tad bit sad just to think of what could happen to Souly.

In her head she made room to justify the whole thing. She said the war was necessary because it would prevent the enemies from coming to our homeland and taking over.

However, what her mouth said and her eyes revealed were as far apart as the east is from the west.

Kobe didn't fret, he knew how strong she was; he guessed it was Mama cat's prayers that protected Souly from what could have happened behind far too many visits to the shack at the end of the track, so surely her prayers could carry Souly to the cat war and back.

The day Souly prepared to leave, Mama Cat sat rocking anxiously on the porch in that old faithful rocker that begged for a fresh coat of paint. Kobe sat at the top of the steps, afraid she would rock right over her own tail.

Trying to act strong, in control, and grownup, careful not to stare, he noticed that she had the small wallet-size picture of Pop Cat that had to be taped on each end, the result of hand held embraces down through the years.

You see, Mama Cat was carrying Kobe in her belly and Souly was only a tot cat when Papa Cat went off to a strange cat war and never made it back.

Kobe remained perched on the top step, clearly lost in space, but alert enough to keep an eye on Mama's tail as she rocked away her heavy heart.

Finally, he knew it was time, the sunflower-yellow cat taxi drove up to the house, which was always considered to be on the Wrong Side of the Track.

Souly came out, slow stepping yet proud, looking braver than brave, cooler than cool.

He bent down, hugged Mama ever so tightly, which stopped that old rocker abruptly, narrowly missing not only her tail but his.

"Mama, what are you gonna do with yourself now that the laundry sold out and left town?" he asked with a concern that pierced the air waves with a disruptive heaviness.

She kissed him gently and smiled that mama cat smile, with one paw touching his whiskers, her way of letting him know that he was now a man cat, all the while clutching Papa Cat's picture in the other paw.

"I am going to rise when the sun rises, bless everyone I meet each and every day, be they kind or unkind. I will rest when the moon appears, announcing its power over the dark sky, and be waiting for you when you come back home to me."

He lovingly kissed her on her head, stroking her salt and pepper hair hoping to console her motherly heart.

"And you, little bro, let's hear it." Said Soley.

Now it was Kobe's turn to embrace this heavy moment, in an effort to make it light.

He meowed in a humble little brother cat kinda way, knowing full well what Souly was expecting to hear,

"Lesson 1 –"Watch what cats do not what cats say."

Souly nodded with approval, laced with that big brotherly pride, "Now what about lesson number 2?" he asked.

Kobe stood upright as if he himself were in the Cat Army as he shouted, much too loudly,

Lesson number 2, "The devil trust the turkey and he flew."

At that very moment they embraced with the biggest big brother little brother hug as Souly whispered in Kobe's ear, "Take care of Mama Cat, you hear?"

Kobe watched Souly slowly step down each of the fifteen rickety steps, as if he were savoring every single move, every single second. It was obvious that by the time he reached the sunflower yellow cat taxi, he was embodied by a heavy, almost hesitant heart of his own.

As if some epiphany struck him unawares, Kobe jumped up so quickly, almost catching his own tail in the old rocker where Mama Cat sat, that had gained even more momentum now,

"Hey Souly, you always told me there were three lessons, but year after year you've told me only two, what the heck is the third lesson?" he shouted.

Souly turned and smiled the biggest, brightest cat smile as he entered the sunflower yellow cat taxi. "I thought you would never ask.

Go to your room and there, right there etched in the mirror, you are sure to see the lesson that I have withheld from you, hoping you would someday ask. There, there you will find life's glorious lesson number 3."

Kobe scratched his head, a bit puzzled as he watched and waited for the sunflower yellow cat taxi to disappear down the street with his beloved brother leaving the Wrong Side of the Track headed for a cat war, while mama cat prayed he would come back alive.

Swiftly, he rushed up the steps, missing Mama Cat's tail, managing to meet her smile, which was filled with a different kind of pride, as if she and Souly knew something he obviously did not.

He leaped in the air, cat style, because that's what cats do, reaching his room in one propelled flight.

Suddenly, something within his gut made him slow down. He guessed he just wanted to relish the moment, kinda take it all in, give it time and space in his head.

His heart was another story – its rapid beat never took a pause; in fact it beat a gazillion thumps a minute.

Taking teeny weenie cat steps now, he could not believe his deep set almond shaped eyes as he gazed into the mirror.

Oh my, how wonderful, how majestic, royal and profound.

There, there it was – the long-awaited life lesson number 3, the one that Souly purposely withheld from him for such a time as this.

He rubbed his eyes just to make sure they were not lying eyes, allowing his heart to quickly dismiss any invasive foolish notion of doubt that ran speedily across his mind.

WOW!

This third lesson was the greatest, sure to outlive all of his nine lives and perhaps, just perhaps, it would propel him to greatness untold.

Etched beneath the mirror's reflection were these marvelous words.

" I am what I see I am...."

Morning's Approach

The day is yet early

A brisk breeze permeates the air

The sun gazes at me through false reflections

Of a misunderstood cloud,

As the water, though not blue, trickles slowly by,

All of this was merely a word for the cricket I heard

Hiding in the brush just before me …

These Eyes

These eyes have viewed the mountains against a sun kissed
sky,

They have witnessed the birth of a title wave that turned into
a summer stream,

These eyes have observed deceit, despair and destruction,

They have lied, cheated, indeed they have even killed with a
sharp deadly stare,

When these eyes saw hurt coming, they made no attempt to
warn my heart,

Alas, when they are closed to rest from the weary day, these
eyes see visions of pain coupled

With loneliness and all the truth that they are unable to see

...

Old Lady Swagger

Old age creeping up on that face,

Line by line, wrinkle by wrinkle,

Spensive creams, moisturizer, ointments, oils and the like,

Doing much of nothing but robbing her blind.

Just as those sneaky unsuspecting years had done,

Didn't matter much whether she dyed that gray hair, blond, black, platinum, rust or red,

Puffiness napping under those eyes like clouds wearing high heel shoes,

Overheard she tried cucumber mask to help out with that disappointing mess,

Bought a pair of Channel sunglasses, darn near covered her entire face, and didn't seem to realize old age doesn't stay in just one place,

From all indications the neck took offense,

Wanted in on some of that old age action,

Started sinking and sagging, hanging and dragging,

Better off kissing those low cut strapless numbers adios

She kept her hair long, healthy and strong,

Wore it most times like a window curtain, swooping to one side,

No doubt, she held that hair accountable for covering half of that growing old face

And a good portion of that neck,

No government cover-up could compare,

In spite of or in lieu of all of that noise going on about old age,

I couldn't help but notice how the

Earth tiptoed in her presence,

Her back is straight,

Her head held high,

85

Still rocks a pair of skintight jeans,

Confidence oozing out of every pore,

No question she's smarter now than she's ever been,

Somewhere between Neiman's and Saks she must have said
to heck with fretting about that

Old age creeping up on her face, line by line, wrinkle by
wrinkle noise,

Old Lady Swagger, embracing the wind!

Adam, Where Are You?

And when it all began, Adam had a directive, marching

orders, a commission and such.

Managed, however, not to do just what he was told.

He acquiesced, and humbly blamed her. After all, she had a

persuasive way about her, with the right look, the right

touch, she could get him to see things her way ...

When he was sought, he hid himself, proclaiming that he was

naked.

He got a bit of a reprieve, although the directive changed,

granting him a sense of knowledge, far different from

wisdom; yet there he goes, all puffed up, riding a wild horse

called free will.

Doesn't seem to have the sense to know that he complicated

the journey,

Now has two roads to choose versus the right one.

Seasons came and seasons have gone, the earth laments,

echoes and shouts from the mountains high and the valleys

low,

Adam, Where are you?

He is once again naked, all the while the earth is clothed in

his shame, the family has been torn apart, foundation

dismantled, babies having babies, no man present to wipe up

the pain.

Patches of hate spread abroad, all dressed up in something

else,

Ice cold hearts running dry, cluttering up the view,

Lies, deceit, deception, neatly framed, hanging proudly upon

the walls of the brain, forever wearing plastered smiles and

invisible daggers that only a warm heart and spiritual

discernment could see.

Trouble with all that is, a warm heart as of late is more of an

anomaly.

No room for ire, not much point in that,

Just listen for my voice moaning among the echoes and

shouts from the mountains high

and the valleys low,

Adam, Where are you?

When Peace Found Me

When Peace finally found me, I was huddled in a fetal position under mountains of volcanic ash,

Far too many eruptions from despair, hurt and shame, the light of day had been shielded by marching bands conducting dark symphonies in my head; everyone knows night has no eyes.

Was there any wonder I was unable to see?

Not sure if it matters now just how long Peace had forgotten my name, Oh but when it finally arrived, I was able to stretch real tall, dismissing the sound of all those cracking bones of hopelessness, making futile attempts to sabotage the moment,

I smiled at Peace from the inside of my once drained and lifeless soul,

Peace came clothed in outstretched arms, happy eyes and a joyous smile it was as if any delay or absence from her presence was clearly on me and not on her.

"Oh, hello, Peace," I whispered loudly from within a resurrecting soul.

'Thank you so very much for hearing my anxious cries.

I was dying a slow death quite rapidly, as you know."

Peace nodded, winked and smiled all at the same time, it seems.

Feeling my limp soul becoming mobile, I eagerly spoke in a humbled tone, "Peace, please do not label me as rude.

If you don't mind, I'm just going to close my eyes but for a moment, and rest in the unfamiliar nature of calm."

Ah, finally I can sleep!

Wings of Love and Laughter

You came into my life riding the wings of love
and laughter

Always had something uplifting, clever, and
kind to say,

Making sure I stayed on Straight Street and
never wore the

Bumps of life as a garment.

Together we nodded at the folly of others,

And speedily found a hole to bury any

Evil that came our way.

In my many moments of silent weakness,

You somehow knew,

As you pulled out your arsenal of wisdom,
style and grace,

Confidently speaking of my infinite strength, and uncircumcised inner power,

Giving sight to the blind spots dancing in my head.

Today, I listened to the birds that sang,

Held tight to the gentle wind that was commissioned to blow,

I found myself reaching for the rays of the morning's sun,

Longing for our fifty years of yesterdays.

And then, out of my heavy heart and empty spaces,

I beckoned my carnal mind to a place called here and now,

Holding tight to your journey in my life.

Reluctantly relinquishing my justified selfishness for you,

My broken heart beats with a melodious rhythm, and a joyous rhyme

Knowing with certainty that you came into my life riding the wings of love

And laughter.

Letting go now, I finally know now,

You fulfilled your God-given gift and purpose,

Spreading your wings of love and laughter for ALL the world to see!

Undying Love,

Mrs. Helen Marie Murry
1/15/2016

He Said

He said, just write, in spite of my pain,

Uncertainty, betrayal and shame,

Never mind the weight of the loneliness I carry around in my
belly,

Or the eyes that only see deceit,

The life of roads that I traveled thinking they were,

Only to find they were not.

He said just write, so, somehow 4:00 a.m. awakens me,

Beckoning me to grab pencil,

find my laptop, pull out paper,

it down and just begin.

Words come pouring out of my head now,

running like innocent children when the school bell rings,

Where are they going?

Some know, perhaps others surely don't.

He said, just write,

Never mind all that noise in my head darkening the light,

Hush to the noise yelling at me, pointing to the road that reads,

Just Quit!

He is a prolific writer,

With footprints on yesterday, today and tomorrow,

He has written and read to Kings and Queens,

Taught, instructed, and lectured to countless many, birthing prolific literary offspring.

He said, I should call myself a writer,

Being careful to be and do just what I say,

He has no clue how it seems much easier to lie down and wait for death to find me,

Death is under time constraints though,

Because rent is due in twenty days.

He said, just write,

I've concluded, he should know,

Obedience is the only dress hanging in my wardrobe,

Clothed in some small semblance of strength and self-worth,

 decide to put death on hold for yet another day,

He said, just write,

So, I...

I just write!

Knocking

I sat there waiting, anticipating, uncertain of many things, certain of others,

The uncertainty was in sync with the rhythm of the trees under the spell of the wind,

The certainty fox trotted with the full knowledge that there would once again be a knock,

I sat this time perched in an easy chair at the door, this chair was no longer easy, and it was now difficult

To sit there all clothed in "what in the world, how in the world did I get here," yet, I sit.

He enters with his key, of course he does, he lives here. Surprised to see me sitting so closely perched

By the door, he speaks, as he always does when entering. We exchange a few words, softening the air

From whatever the heck was filling the air. And then, he goes and sits, with anticipation and certainty.

My mind was filled with nothingness, as I sat back a bit in that easy chair, chocking on uneasiness. I

Suddenly hear what seemed like an army of feet coming up the wooden stirs, and then, before I could

claim any lucid thought, I hear, BAM BAM, BAM, Police!

Removing my rump from that easy chair that was never easy to begin with, I did as they commanded,

Opened the door and stepped out. However, not before SHOUTING,

"There are NO weapons in the house." Five armed police, ready, perhaps even

Eager to shoot away the day, clearly needed to be assured of at least that fact.

That was yesterday, that was seven years ago, that was three years ago, but it is not today. Today, I

Wonder why does trouble follow him so? Why, I wonder, do I sit at the door of anticipation and

Uncertainty, perched upon an easy chair, that was never easy in the first place,

Waiting for his trouble to come knocking, certain to disrupt my heartbeat?

If Kindness Had a Color

If Kindness had a color, we suspect it

Would be aqua, like the gentle whispering ocean waves,

Perhaps it would embrace multiple colors

Like the rainbow, tiptoeing across the humble naked sky,

What if kindness were the highest mountain top

All dressed up with green trees dancing to and fro,

Then again kindness just might be purple, like the flowering
lavender plant

Spitting a magnificent scent, that leaves a smile frolicking in
the wind,

If kindness had a color, it would surely be transparent and
pure, like

The summer breeze blowing nuggets of peace and love, over
here, and over there,

We have put our heads together, oddly enough came to a meeting of the minds,

Not a nay could be found, it is unanimous, you must know,

If Kindness had a color it would be Chris Cox, all decked out in bright colors of

Happiness, Helpfulness and a Willingness to extend a hand and pure heart to everyone blessed to have met him.

Thank you, Chris, for sharing your world of kindness with all of us.

Written following the passing of Chris Cox, a magnificent TSA agent, Dallas Love Field Airport
/2016

Breathing

Suddenly Charleston, with all its movement, horse-led buggies, click, clack, click, clack, and water and energy and dancing with years gone by every step you take, like a child, yet unable to express the childlike glee, be still my heart, just for a moment…Ahhh

Somehow Charleston begins to suck the life from me. Okay, I find no fault in her spender, ocean breeze and sunsets!

Not sure why the thought of a scab over a wound comes to mind. Like a sore forever in route of healing, Wondering now if that analogy is of me or Charleston… or both me and Charleston.

I breathe, being fragmented and broken in so many places, takes healing awhile to catch up with wholeness, perhaps breathing is the answer,

So, I breathe, wondering if Charleston will do the same!

Altered Dreams

She was going on her fifth husband, now approaching her sixty-eighth birthday,

Looking back over the landscape of her life she no longer smiled at memories

That she once cherished.

Her long, thick blond hair hid gray strands, that only she and a magnifying glass could see,

Happy times were sandwiched someplace amid the wrinkles on her neck,

And the reoccurring thought of plastic surgery.

Her dreams were faded now, no longer bright and airy like rainbows

Showing up across a peaceful sky.

In fact, dreams were replaced with quick ten-minute naps that rushed in just as quickly as she sat down, lying down was no longer a prerequisite that beckoned sleep to come.

This next husband didn't need to be tall, or dark or even handsome.

It wasn't necessary for him to be wealthy or successful.

He could even be in his seventies, or early eighties might do.

Breath and britches, that's where the line had been drawn,

He had to be breathing and wearing britches. Time clearly has a way

Of altering dreams, shifting thoughts and stripping off haughty airs.

It had all come down to low-level realities, what's important is to see a sunrise and someone to share and confirm it indeed rose.

Someone to occupy the space in the room,
drowning the noise of loneliness completely out.

If laughter came to visit, and she hoped it would, it would find her

And her fifth husband laughing at something as simple as an all-out search

For missing car keys or a sock that the dryer ate.

Yeah, she no longer considered extended periods of unleashed bliss and long

Walks on the sandy beach. If memory serves, she buried
those dreams years ago, about

The time she became totally preoccupied with how to
effectively hide crow's feet.

Growing old is not what it's cracked up to be, it's so much
more,

like altered dreams rich in simple things,

like waking up and being glad you did!

Our Letter of Love to Brooke

You came to us as a gift from God
Riding high on the wings of hope for the future,

We watched you smile
And remembered what happy looked like,

We laughed with you
And danced with the beauty of being joyful,

We excitedly listened to your hopes and dreams
As we dusted off our own lazy possibilities,

You listened to the birds sing
Forcing us to hear their song,

You reached for the stars
And we noticed their light,

You tiptoed to the sound of the gentle wind

And we learned to appreciate the breeze,

You threw kisses to the rising sun

Reminding us to salute the wonder of a new day,

Brooke, collectively we confirm that you are destined for goodness and greatness

As we

Thank You for the Present of your Presence in our lives.

Your Loving family,

Looking For Yesterday

At 95 years of age her mind was sharp,
humorously crisp, laughter found its way in
every conversation,

Her trusted body betrayed her , legs that use to
be strong, lean and long subtracted inches from
a lady that once was considered tall,

Both knees were replaced, granting her
permission to continue going up and down
those steep stairs,

No matter what, at least twice a week she
would get in that old Honda Accord that looked
close to brand new and drive the fifteen
minutes to Delray, a section of South West
Detroit that housed her vivid memories of
yesterday.

The Lebanese-American poet Kahlil Gibran
wrote, "You talk when you cease to be at peace
with your thoughts."

Clearly, she was no longer at peace with her thoughts of yesterday as all of her contemporaries, siblings, old neighbors, friends and her beloved husband John had crossed over to the other side.

It was an honor for me to listen when she spoke, she seemed to figure what purpose did yesterday serve all wrapped up there in her head, dancing on vinyl records all alone? I figured I wanted to join her in this dance for as long as I possibly could.

Ironically, her visits to Delray somehow gave her strength to live another day that was bathed in nothing but her longing for yesterday. It didn't make much sense, defied logic to me.

My thread was woven with her yesterday, I knew first hand of Peterson Street, the sunny days that rang bells of simpler times, children's laughter and old folk's secrets.

She had a 32 year head start on me though, and I went as far along with her as I could, able to nod and imagine her fields of joy. The fact is, she was always a part of my yesterdays, in some form, always a good fashion.

It turns out she was waiting for just the right time to let go of yesterday and surrender to the wind.
I spoke with her the morning that came to be her last, it hangs on me often like ill fitted clothing, cramping my style, disrupting my stride.

What am I to do with all the talks she left me hugging the empty hole she managed to leave in my soul?

Gray hair crowning, more like covering my head now, a daily reminder, my days are getting shorter too...

Well, if ever I make it back to Delray, all covered
in left over particles of what used to be,
I'll make it a point of spending a bit of time
driving around looking for yesterday,

Somehow...
It makes sense to me now!

Reverie

Life's journey has whispered many things in my ears with situations that literally took my breath away. Life has also been kind, blessing me with people, most of whom left cemented footprints of love.

The take away, I suspect could be, when we surrender to that place of peace clothed from head to toe in our trusting that God, "makes it all right even when it feels all wrong," then the doors of our heart spring open with a high step, allowing Joy to come in moving us Beyond the Tears.

About The Author

Joyce E. Green began her literary journey working as a writer for a community paper in her hometown of Detroit, Michigan while in college. One might think her love for writing took a back seat to a professional career as a real estate broker licensed in three states, focusing on business and obtaining a MBA degree, however, her writing never ceased.

Joyce is a published poet now surrendering to her literary passion. Writing a collection of short stories and poems was a seamless transition from the often noisy business world. In addition to writing and real estate she is a public speaker advocating and bringing awareness to mental illness, which affects 1 in 5 families. Joyce is a member of NAMI (National Alliance on Mental Illness) and a volunteer at MUSC Institute of Psychiatry Patient Family Partnership Council.

Over the years Joyce has lived in several states as well as Kingston, Jamaica, she now calls Charleston, SC home.

Made in the USA
Columbia, SC
27 February 2018